WILD FLOWERS
OF SPAIN AND PORTUGAL

WILD FLOWERS
OF SPAIN
AND PORTUGAL

by

A. W. TAYLOR

1972
CHATTO & WINDUS
LONDON

Published by
Chatto & Windus Ltd
40/42 William IV Street
London W.C.2.

*

Clarke, Irwin and Co. Ltd
Toronto

ISBN 0 7011 1917 9

Printed in Great Britain by
Bookprint International Limited   .

INTRODUCTION

A mere two days' motoring separate the green, cool, and rain-soaked Atlantic coast of Spain from the semi-desert conditions around Almeria on the Mediterranean, where the rainfall may be only 200 mm. in a year. And, between Atlantic and Mediterranean, lies Spain, with its high plateaux, great Sierras and deep rich river valleys, all showing wide variations in temperatures, rainfall, soil, and vegetation.

Cut off from the rest of Europe by the great wall of the Pyrenees, and further isolated by range after range of Sierras, the native plants of Spain and Portugal have been to a large extent sheltered from outside influences. This is shown by the fact that a quarter of the very large number of the naturally occurring species of the Iberian Peninsula are endemics; and of the mountain plants, there are many which are confined to one, or a few Sierras. Even in the Mediterranean coastal zone, many Western Mediterranean species are found which are either restricted to Spain, or, in some cases, to North Africa also.

To this complicated and fascinating blend of climatic and geographical influences which have produced the flora of the Iberian Peninsula, must be added the alterations and the additions made by man. The effects of untold centuries of wood cutting for fuel, and uncontrolled grazing, particularly by goats, are obvious in the huge deforested areas where the "garigue" or "steppe" types of vegetation have taken over. An equally obvious effect of human activity has been the introduction and extensive cultivation of such plants as the Olive the Almond, the Vine and the Orange. All these have now been cultivated in Spain and Portugal for so long that they are part of the Iberian scene, and the precise period of their introduction is forgotten.

Nor would we be without the numerous and exotic garden plants, so brilliantly gay and colourful, which are widely grown and naturalized along the coasts.

It is hoped that this little book will introduce the interested traveller to examples of some of the lovely flowers which will interest and, perhaps, puzzle him on his holidays in these most beautiful countries.

ABBREVIATIONS

cm.	=	centimetre (0·39 in.)
m.	=	metre (39·37 in.)
mm.	=	millimetre (0·04 in.)
sp.	=	species
ssp.	=	sub-species
var.	=	variety

Inches

Centimetres

CONTENTS

Introduction   PAGE   v
Abbreviations   vi

FAMILY   SPECIES

Liliaceae   Allium roseum   15
                        Allium subhirsutum   92
                        Aloe arborescens   61
                        Asphodelus aestivus   57
                        Asphodelus albus   95
                        Asphodelus fistulosus   14
                        Dipcadi serotinum   16
                        Fritillaria hispanica   10
                        Fritillaria lusitanica   13
                        Gagea hispanica   11

Amaryllidaceae   Agave americana   20
                        Leucojum trichophyllum   96
                        Narcissus asturiensis   21
                        Narcissus bulbocodium   63
                        Narcissus bulbocodium var. citrinus   69
                        Narcissus minutiflorus   19
                        Narcissus nevadensis   34
                        Narcissus nobilis   99
                        Narcissus papyraceus   72
                        Narcissus triandrus   31

Iridaceae   Crocus nevadensis   26
                        Gladiolus segetum   22
                        Iris florentina   17
                        Iris planifolia   18
                        Iris sisyrinchium   23

Orchidaceae   Ophrys tenthredinifera   42
                        Orchis laxiflora   43
                        Serapias pseudocordigera   38

Aristolochiaceae   Aristolochia baetica   35

Aizoaceae   Carpobrotus acinaciformis   39

Ranunculaceae   Anemone palmata   24
                        Ranunculus acetosellaefolius   30

Paeoniaceae   Paeonia broteroi   47

VII

FAMILY	SPECIES	PAGE
Cruciferae	Lobularia maritima	77
	Matthiola sinuata	68
	Moricandia arvensis	64.
Rosaceae	Prunus dulcis	94
	Prunus prostrata	50
Leguminosae	Acacia longifolia	51
	Anthyllis cytisoides	88
	Astragalus lusitanicus	85
	Ceratonia siliqua	93
	Cercis siliquastrum	59
	Cytisus multiflorus	80
	Erinacea anthyllis	27
	Genista cinerea	32
	Genista equisetiformis	58
	Lathyrus tingitanus	29
	Lupinus angustifolius	54
	Medicago marina	62
	Ononis natrix	55
	Spartium junceum	90
	Ulex minor	89
Oxalidaceae	Oxalis pes-caprae	66
Euphorbiaceae	Euphorbia characias	33
Violaceae	Viola cazorlensis	82
Cistaceae	Cistus ladaniferus	98
	Cistus monspeliensis	84
	Cistus populifolius	60
	Halimium atriplicifolium	81
	Helianthemum apenninum	44
Cactaceae	Opuntia ficus-indica	45
Ericaceae	Erica arborea	73
Oleaceae	Olea europaea	12
Gentianaceae	Gentiana verna	25
Apocynaceae	Nerium oleander	83
	Vinca difformis	52
Convolvulaceae	Convolvulus althaeoides	86
	Convolvulus lanuginosus	49
Boraginaceae	Anchusa azurea	56
	Borago officinalis	53
	Echium lycopsis	91
	Lithospermum purpureo-coeruleum	87

FAMILY	SPECIES	PAGE
Labiatae	Lavandula dentata	37
	Lavandula pedunculata	67
	Phlomis purpurea	70
	Rosmarinus officinalis	89
Solanaceae	Hyoscyamus albus	40
	Nicotiana glauca	65
Scrophulariaceae	Digitalis obscura	71
Compositae	Carthamus arborescens	79
	Chrysanthemum coronarium	78
	Chrysanthemum hispanicum	97
	Helichrysum stoechas	74
	Odontospermum maritimum	75
	Scolymus hispanicus	41
Palmae	Chamaerops humilis	28
Gramineae	Arundo donax	76
Araceae	Arisarum vulgare	46
Pinaceae	Pinus pinea	36
Fagaceae	Quercus suber	48

*   *   *

Map of the Area   101

Alphabetical index of the plants illustrated with Latin
    and English names   102 and 103

Fritillaria hispanica

Family: *Liliaceae*

Spanish representative of a genus of bulbous plants which carry bell-shaped flowers often known as "Snake's-head". This species is usually 30 cm. high and the leaves are rather wide. The drooping flower is large and varies much in colour, though chequering is rare, and the colour is often of a dull maroon with green striping. Often found on stony hillsides among low-growing bushes such as Cistus, Genistas and Lavenders. Widely distributed throughout Spain. (Sierra Nevada) *April–June*.

Gagea hispanica

Family: *Liliaceae*

A small bulbous plant growing up to 12 cm. high. Leaves narrow, and the brilliant yellow starry flowers borne in a cluster on a single stem. This Spanish plant is found from sea level, where it flowers from February–March, to a height of up to 2500 m. The specimen figured was blooming at 2500 m. on the Sierra Nevada in May.

Olea europaea (Olive)

Family: *Oleaceae*

The Olive tree, part of human life and civilizations in the Mediterranean area since the dawn of history, is grown and naturalized from S. W. Portugal along the entire Mediterranean coast. Its graceful trees, grey barked and reaching a height of up to 10 m., carry lance-shaped leaves, grey-green above and white beneath: the clusters of small white flowers are followed by the green or black fruits. (Granada) *May–June*.

Fritillaria lusitanica

Family: *Liliaceae*

A bulbous plant possessing the peculiar fascination of the genus. The drooping bells of a dark maroon without, with variable chequering, and shining yellow within, are carried on stems 30–40 cm. high. The leaves are narrow, long, and of a bluish-green. This species is found in Portugal, and grows in open woodland and maquis. The specimen figured was growing among Cistus ladaniferus. (Southern Portugal) *February–April.*

Asphodelus fistulosus

Family: *Liliaceae*

This small but very handsome Asphodel, with narrow leaves and branched stems up to 60 cm. high, carries spikes of white or pinkish flowers. It is found along the whole Mediterranean coast and prefers dry or sandy places. (Nr. Almeria) *March–June*.

Allium roseum (Rose Garlic)

Family: *Liliaceae*

One of the most beautiful of the European Garlics, carrying rounded heads of large pale rose-coloured flowers on 20–40 cm. high stems. Leaves broadly linear. Occurs throughout the Mediterranean region, and frequently inland, growing on roadsides and in fields. (Foothills of Sierra Cazorla) *April–June*.

Dipcadi serotinum

Family: *Liliaceae*

An inconspicuous and rather uncommon bulbous plant, with narrow leaves and 10–30 cm. stems carrying golden-brown bell-shaped flowers. Grows in dry stony places from sea level to 2000 m. (Gredos mountains, Central Spain) *May–July*.

Iris florentina

Family: *Iridaceae*

This Iris, possibly of hybrid origin, is widely distributed in the Mediterranean region and inland. From clumps of broad sword-shaped leaves spring stems 40–60 cm. high, bearing 2–4 large white flowers, sometimes veined with blue. On roadsides and stony hillsides. (Southern Portugal) *February–April.*

17

Iris planifolia

Family: *Iridaceae*

The only Western representative of the fabulous Juno group of Irises, whose main area of distribution lies in Turkey, Iran, and Iraq. I. planifolia, with its broad bluish-green leaves and large silvery mauve flowers carried on 15–25 cm. stems, is one of the glories of earliest Spring in Andalucia, where it is locally abundant on limestone Sierras. (Andalucia) *January–March*.

Narcissus minutiflorus

Family: *Amaryllidaceae*

The smallest of all Jonquils, with flowers only 10 mm. in diameter, from 1–4 on a stem. Leaves round.
Grows in semi-shaded rock gullies in the extreme South of Portugal and Spain. *January–March.*

Agave americana (Century Plant)

Family: *Amaryllidaceae*

This Mexican plant, introduced and now widely naturalized in the Mediterranean area, produces large rosettes of thick bluish-green spiny-edged leaves. After 10–15 years huge flowering stems of up to 10 m. length carry branches of green flowers, after which the rosette dies. Grows around houses, on rocks by the sea, and by roadsides. (Andalucia) *May–August*.

Narcissus asturiensis

Family: *Amaryllidaceae*

This, the smallest of the trumpet daffodils, reaches a height of only 5–10 cm. It is of a concolourous golden yellow, with constricted trumpet expanded at the margin. In spite of ruthless collection, this charming little daffodil is still locally abundant in the mountains of Northern Portugal and Spain. (Picos de Europa) *March–May*.

Gladiolus segetum

Family: *Iridaceae*

The common wild Gladiolus of the South, with handsome 40–80 cm. high one-sided spikes of 6–10 rose purple flowers. Grows abundantly in cultivated fields, among corn, and in Olive groves. (Estremadura) *April–June.*

Iris sisyrinchium (Barbary Nut)

Family: *Iridaceae*

A small delicate Iris, of a clear light blue with white throat and gold markings. The flowers are carried on 10–30 cm. stems in groups of 2–4. The flowers are of short life, lasting only a day before fading and being replaced by others. Leaves narrow. This Southern species may be found amongst rocks and in the sand at the edge of the Mediterranean, but also grows in great numbers along roadsides and amongst rocky outcrops inland. (Estremadura) *February–May*.

Anemone palmata (Palmate Anemone)

Family: *Ranunculaceae*

Basal leaves rounded, with 3–5 broad and shallow lobes. Stem leaves at the base show 3–5 deeply cut segments. The flower stems, 10–30 cm. high, carry large golden-yellow flowers streaked with reddish-brown on the reverse of the petals, which vary in number from 10–18. A beautiful Anemone of the far S.W. of Spain, growing on hills, on road verges, and at the edges of cultivated ground, usually on limestone. (Andalucia) *February–April.*

24

Gentiana verna (Spring Gentian)

Family: *Gentianaceae*

This, one of the most beautiful members of its genus, decorates with its brilliant blue starry flowers many of the high sierras of Spain, from the Sierra Nevada in the far South, to the Picos de Europa in the North; not usually found below an altitude of 1500 m. (Lerida) *April–June.*

Crocus nevadensis

Family: *Iridaceae*

This rare and beautiful Crocus of the far South is, as the name implies, found on the Sierra Nevada where it grows at an altitude of 2500 m. Leaves and flowers appear together, and the starry white flowers, veined with lilac to a greater or less degree, follow the edge of the melting snows on the mountainsides. (Sierra Nevada) *May–June.*

Erinacea anthyllis (Hedgehog Broom)

Family: *Leguminosae*

A dense, often rounded shrub, 20–50 cm. high, very spiny, with inconspicuous leaves which fall early, and violet coloured flowers arising usually in pairs from the upper leaf axils. Young shoots and flower calyces silvery hairy. This very beautiful shrub is found in the Sierra Nevada and a few other Southern Spanish Sierras, though it is also found in North Africa and as.a great rarity in the Spanish Pyrenees. (Sierra Nevada) *May–June.*

27

Chamaerops humilis (Dwarf Fan Palm)

Family: *Palmae*

The only native European Palm, confined to the Mediterranean coast in the far South.

The whole plant is dwarf, with short stem, the leaves fan-shaped with 12–15 stiff narrow segments, and the flower heads in dense clusters among the leaves. Grows in dry rocky places, often on hillsides. (Andalucia) *March–June.*

Lathyrus tingitanus (Tangier Pea)

Family: *Leguminosae*

A Vetch of scrambling habit, the lower leaves narrow and unsegmented, the upper with 2–4 pairs of narrow leaflets. Carries heads of 1–2 large crimson flowers. Grows in sandy or stony places, at roadsides and in fields in the western Mediterranean and North Africa. (Andalucia) *March–May*.

Ranunculus acetosellaefolius

Family: *Ranunculaceae*

A rare and beautiful white mountain buttercup, confined to the Sierra Nevada, where it grows and flowers in the wet high screes soon after the melting of the snows in May and June. From a basal rosette of widely lance-shaped leaves with waved edges and of a smooth grey-green, spring the golden-centred white flowers, carried singly on 10 cm. high stems. (Sierra Nevada.)

Narcissus triandrus (Angel's Tears)

Family: *Amaryllidaceae*

In this miniature Narcissus species, 1–3 flowers, in which the perianth segments are reflexed, are carried on stems 10–20 cm. high. This beautiful and variable species shows a wide range of colour from white to orange, and has its main distribution in Western Spain and Portugal. (Picos de Europa) *March–May*.

Genista cinerea

Family: *Leguminosae*

A grey-green, spineless, and much branched shrub, 1–2 m. high with narrow leaves and clusters of 1–5 yellow flowers. Grows in dry rocky places of limestone. Western Mediterranean and North Africa. (Almeria) *March–June*.

Euphorbia characias

Family: *Euphorbiaceae*

A stout plant, with many 30–80 cm. stems rising from a woody base, carrying narrow leaves and terminal flower heads distinguished by their dark purplish glands. A common plant of stony hillsides. (Gerona) *March–May*.

Narcissus nevadensis

Family: *Amaryllidaceae*

This very rare and remarkable daffodil is not only the most southerly of all the larger trumpet daffodils, but is unique in bearing two or sometimes three flowers on one stem. Grows at an altitude of from 1500–2000 m. in damp or boggy conditions on the Sierra Nevada. *April–June.*

Aristolochia baetica

Family: *Aristolochiaceae*

A climbing plant bearing heart-shaped leaves and dull purple flowers,
U-shaped and funnel-like. Not uncommon in Southern Andalucia,
where it scrambles over shrubs in open woodland. *February–April.*

Pinus pinea (Stone Pine, Umbrella Pine)

Family: *Pinaceae*

This very familiar pine of the Mediterranean area grows to a height of up to 30 m., and is recognized by its flat-topped crown. The long trunk is brown, and scales off in patches to leave orange-coloured areas. Bears very large cones. (Andalucia) *April–May*.

Lavandula dentata

Family: *Labiatae*

One of the Lavenders of the Spanish Mediterranean and North Africa. The narrow leaves have toothed margins and the flower heads are very compact. Grows on the rocks and cliffs of the sea coast. (Alicante) *February–May*.

Serapias pseudocordigera (S. vomeracea)

Family: *Orchidaceae*

A tall orchid of extraordinary appearance and sombre colouring. The stout stem is red-spotted at the base, grows up to 45 cm. and carries 2–10 large flowers with pale brownish-red hood and long three-lobed lip of an even darker hue. Occurs along both Atlantic and Mediterranean coasts of Spain, growing in damp meadows and on hillsides. (Picos de Europa) *March–May*.

Carpobrotus acinaciformis (Red Hottentot Fig)

Family: *Aizoaceae*

This handsome succulent plant, a South African native, has been naturalized for so long on the coasts of Spain and Portugal that it forms an important part of the coastal flora, with its sprawling woody stems bearing mats of fleshy dark green leaves and brilliant carmine flowers 10 cm. in diameter. (Alicante) *March–June.*

Hyoscyamus albus (White Henbane)

Family: *Solanaceae*

A low-growing plant with large, coarse, more or less rounded leaves, and flowers of a pale yellow. Common in waste places. (Alicante) *March–June*.

Scolymus hispanicus

Family: *Compositae*

A very spiny plant, allied to the thistles, which grows to a height of about 1 m. The yellow flowers are carried in the axils of the leaves. Grows in waste places and on roadsides in sandy or stony ground. (Granada) *April–July.*

Ophrys tenthredinifera (Sawfly Orchid)

Family: *Orchidaceae*

One of the most beautiful of all the Ophrys species, with bright pink sepals and golden-yellow lip with central brown area. 3–8 flowers are carried on 10–30 cm. stems. Grows on limestone hills and outcrops and flowers from February to April. (Andalucia.)

Orchis laxiflora (Loose-flowered Orchid)

Family: *Orchidaceae*

A graceful orchid, 30–60 cm. high, with narrow leaves and spikes of 6–20 widely spaced flowers which vary in colour from reddish-purple to violet. The broad lip has a central white area. A rather uncommon orchid favouring poorly drained meadows and marshes. (Estremadura) *May–June.*

Helianthemum apenninum (White Rockrose)

Family: *Cistaceae*

A small shrubby plant, woody at the base, and growing to a height of up to 20 cm. The leaves are narrow, whitish and downy, and the flowers white with yellow centres. Grows on limestone from sea level up to 1500 m. in the mountains. (Almeria) *April–June.*

Opuntia ficus-indica (Prickly Pear)

Family: *Cactaceae*

This Mexican plant, introduced long ago to the Mediterranean area, is now so widely cultivated and naturalized that its striking appearance has become part of the Mediterranean scene. A fleshy plant, made up of many oval joints, it is very prickly. The flowers are yellow and the fruits a dark purplish red. Flowers May to July. (Andalucia.)

Arisarum vulgare (Friar's Cowl)

Family: *Araceae*

The most widespread and most charming of the Mediterranean arums, growing to a height of about 10 cm. or less, with oval lobed leaves, and hooded flowers of green and purple.
Common in a very wide variety of habitats. (Andalucia) *January–April*.

Paeonia broteroi

Family: *Paeoniaceae*

One of the glories of the Sierras of Portugal and Southern Spain, this species is found on rocky hillsides in low scrub, or at the edges of pinewoods, up to an altitude of about 1500 m. It reaches a height of about a metre, and its deeply cut dark green leaves have a reddish tinge. The large and very handsome golden-centred flowers vary in colour from pink to a rich dark red. (Sierra de Cazorla) *April–June*.

Quercus suber (Cork Oak)

Family: *Fagaceae*

A tree growing to 5–15 m. in height, with very thick fissured bark which is stripped every 10 years to yield commercial cork. Leaves oval and leathery in texture, greyish beneath, and sometimes spiny edged. Grown extensively on poor acid soils in the Western Mediterranean region of Portugal and Spain. (Andalucia) *April–May*.

Convolvulus lanuginosus

Family: *Convolvulaceae*

A narrow-leaved silvery plant with 10–30 cm. stems carrying crowded clusters of white flowers tinged with rose. This graceful little plant grows on dry stony hillsides, often as a component of the garigue vegetation. (Andalucia) *April–July.*

Prunus prostrata

Family: *Rosaceae*

A dwarf Prunus, often entirely prostrate, forming mats of branching woody stems hugging rock faces and boulders. Leaves small and oval, and the rose-coloured flowers borne singly or in pairs. Grows at an altitude of up to 1200 m. on the Sierra Nevada. *May–June.*

Acacia longifolia

Family: *Leguminosae*

One of the numerous Mimosas cultivated and sometimes naturalized in Southern Spain and Portugal. This small tree, with blue-green willow-like leaves, is a rapidly growing species and is often used for stabilization and reclamation of sandy dunes at the coast. The yellow flowers are carried in elongated clusters. (S. Portugal) *January–March.*

51

Vinca difformis

Family: *Apocynaceae*

A trailing perennial with thick dark green leaves in pairs, and large flowers of a pale blue or near white. Grows at streamsides and in shady places. (Alicante) *February–May.*

Borago officinalis (Common Borage)

Family: *Boraginaceae*

A hairy and rather coarse plant, with broadly oval leaves, and stout flowering stems carrying bright blue starry flowers on long stalks. Common in waste places, at roadsides, and field edges (Alicante) *April–August*.

Lupinus angustifolius

Family: *Leguminosae*

A frequent plant of sandy places near the sea. Grows to a height of 40–50 cm., has leaves deeply divided into narrow segments, and carries heads of dark blue flowers. (Portugal). *February–May*.

Ononis natrix

Family: *Leguminosae*

A low-growing bushy plant with sticky leaves, carrying rather large deep yellow pea flowers, fading to a brownish-red. Often found in sandy or rocky places near the sea, but also ascending to 1500 m. in the mountains. Usually found on limestone. (Alicante) *March–June*.

Anchusa azurea

Family: *Boraginaceae*

A very handsome plant, with hairy lance-shaped leaves and tall loose sprays of bright blue flowers, reaching a height of up to 1 m. Common in fields, roadsides and waste places. (Badajoz) *April–July.*

Asphodelus aestivus (Asphodel)

Family: *Liliaceae*

A large Asphodel with narrow leaves up to 1 m. long, and a tall much branched stem of up to 1½ m. height, carrying heads of white flowers veined with brown. A common and handsome feature of rocky places and hills, at the coast and inland. (Andalucia) *February–May*.

Genista equisetiformis

Family: *Leguminosae*

A low dense-growing shrub up to 50 cm. high, whose green, almost leafless stems carry spherical heads of tightly packed golden flowers. Grows in arid stony places in Southern Spain. (Andalucia) *April–June.*

Cercis siliquastrum

Family: *Leguminosae*

This, the Judas tree, is widely cultivated and sometimes naturalized throughout the whole Mediterranean area. It reaches a height of 4–6 m. and carries large clusters of handsome rose-purple pea flowers on its bare branches in early Spring. (Cordoba) *March–May*.

Cistus populifolius

Family: *Cistaceae*

A large-flowered white Cistus, aromatic, sticky, and growing to a height of 1½ m. Leaves heart-shaped and pointed. Widely distributed in Spain, and often a common constituent of the "Matorral" on rocky hillsides and in dry places. (Badajoz) *March–May*.

Aloe arborescens

Family: *Liliaceae*

From large rosettes of fleshy blue-green leaves, spear-shaped and spiny, arise flower spikes up to 90 cm. high, carrying handsome red flowers. Not an indigenous plant, but widely grown for hedging purposes, and frequently naturalized. (Andalucia) *February–April.*

Medicago marina (Sea Medick)

Family: *Leguminosae*

A low-growing spreading plant with white-downy leaves, making mats on sand-dunes on the coast. Flowers bright lemon-yellow in tight clusters. (Portugal) *February–May*.

Narcissus bulbocodium

Family: *Amaryllidaceae*

A miniature daffodil, growing to a height of 10–20 cm., characterized by the relatively large bulbous trumpet (corona), and the much reduced perianth segments. (Hoop Petticoat Daffodil). This little daffodil shows great variability in size, colour, shape and leaf, so that many varietal names have been used in description. N. bulbocodium has its home in the Iberian Peninsula but also occurs in Western France and North Africa. (Serra de Arrabida, Portugal) *February–April*.

Moricandia arvensis

Family: *Cruciferae*

Found near the coast, but extending well inland, this striking plant carries its large violet coloured flowers on 50 cm. high, branched stems. Its rounded leaves are thick, hairless and of a grey-green colour. Grows on stony banks, roadsides, and on cliffs, in Southern Spain and North Africa. (Andalucia) *February–May.*

Nicotiana glauca

Family: *Solanaceae*

A straggling shrub, 2–3 m. high, with woody stems, egg-shaped blue-green leaves, and long tubular yellow flowers. Originating in S. America, N. glauca has for long been widely naturalized throughout the Mediterranean area. It grows in waste places and on dry rocky banks and hillsides near the sea. Flowers over much of the year. (Andalucia.)

Oxalis pes-caprae

Family: *Oxalidaceae*

The Bermuda Buttercup, a common and beautiful plant of the roadsides and fields of Southern Spain and Portugal is for agriculturalists a serious weed. From tufts of long-stalked bright green trefoil-shaped leaves spring 15–20 cm. stalks carrying sprays of bright lemon-yellow flowers. (Andalucia) *February–May*.

Lavandula pedunculata

Family: *Labiatae*

This handsome lavender, resembling the common L. stoechas of the Mediterranean coast, grows to a height of about 60 cm. The leaves are narrow, with inrolled margins and the whole plant is grey-downy. The flowers are carried in short densely-packed terminal spikes of a dark purple colour, with violet-purple bracts, and are topped by a cluster of bracts of the same violet-purple colour, longer than those of L. stoechas. (Gredos mountains) *May–August*.

Matthiola sinuata (Sea Stock)

Family: *Cruciferae*

A plant of very wide geographical distribution, with grey, wavy-edged leaves, and loose heads of pale lilac flowers, growing to a height of 40 cm. Always found near the sea, M. sinuata grows in sand or among rocks. (Andalucia) *February–May*.

Narcissus bulbocodium var. citrinus

Family: *Amaryllidaceae*

This very beautiful Bulbocodium has flowers of a pale lemon yellow, 35–50 mm. long. It may be associated with the more common golden yellow N. Bulbocodium, or may be unmixed over large areas. Found in Western Spain from the Cantabrian mountains in the North to the Gredos mountains in mid-Spain. (Gredos mountains) *February–April*.

Phlomis purpurea

Family: *Labiatae*

A handsome shrub growing to a height of up to 1½ m., with lance-shaped leaves toothed at the edges and woolly below. The soft pink flowers are carried in whorls up the numerous stout stems. Grows on hillsides in Southern Spain, often in the company of Cistus species. (Sierra de Cordoba) *April–June*.

Digitalis obscura

Family: *Scrophulariaceae*

This, the finest of the Spanish Foxgloves, grows to a height of 60–80 cm. Its narrow leaves are of a dark and glossy green and it produces spikes of beautiful red and orange flowers. Although never abundant, it has a wide distribution in the Sierras of Southern Spain. (Sierra de Cazorla) *May–July.*

Narcissus papyraceus (Paper-White Narcissus)

Family: *Amaryllidaceae*

Leaves broad and blue-green in colour. Long stems, 30 cm. high, carry 5–20 snow-white and very sweetly scented flowers. Grows at roadsides, on stony or rocky hills, and on cultivated ground. (Andalucia) *January–March.*

72

Erica arborea (Tree Heath)

Family: *Ericaceae*

A very tall and much branched Heather carrying dense clusters of small white or pinkish flowers. Usually reaches a height of 1–4 m., though this height may be exceeded. Locally extremely abundant in the Western Mediterranean area. (Sierra de Ronda). *February–April.*

Helichrysum stoechas

Family: *Compositae*

A bushy plant up to 30 cm. high, with erect stems carrying narrow white woolly leaves and small globular flower heads of bright yellow "everlasting" flowers. The flowers have a characteristic curry-like smell. Common in rocky and sandy places. (Almeria) *February–April.*

Odontospermum maritimum (Asteriscus maritimus)

Family: *Compositae*

A coastal plant, forming dense rounded clumps of dark green spoon-shaped leaves, covered with the large golden yellow flowers. One of the finest of the cliff-growing plants of the Mediterranean coast. (Andalucia) *February–May*.

Arundo donax (Giant Reed)

Family: Gramineae

A tall woody-stemmed reed, 2–5 m. high, springing from underground
tuberous stems. Flowers feathery, becoming silvery in colour. This,
the tallest European grass, is grown to form windbreaks, and the
dried cut stems are used in mat and basket making, as fishing rods,
and many other ways. (Andalucia) *August–October*.

Lobularia maritima (Sweet Alison)

Family: *Cruciferae*

A small spreading perennial with narrow silvery leaves and clustered heads of white scented flowers. Very common on sands and rocks on the coast. (Andalucia) *February–July*.

Chrysanthemum coronarium (Crown Daisy)

Family: *Compositae*

Another of the brilliant roadside flowers of Southern Spain. The leaves are deeply divided, and the large flowers, varying in colour from near white to deepest golden, are carried on 80 cm high stems. (Cordoba) *April–July*.

Carthamus arborescens

Family: *Compositae*

A tall Southern Thistle, with very spiny bright green leaves, and tall flowering stems up to 2 m. high, bearing large yellow flowers. Common in dry stony places in Southern Spain and North Africa. (Andalucia) *April–July*.

Cytisus multiflorus (Spanish White Broom)

Family: *Leguminosae*

An erect and much branched shrub reaching a height of up to 3 m. The stems carry many clusters of white flowers, and the leaves are simple or trifoliate with silvery hairs. Grows on dry hills in Spain and Portugal. (Caceres) *February–May.*

Halimium atriplicifolium

Family: *Cistaceae*

A very handsome Cistus-like shrub, reaching a height of about 1m.
The grey-green elliptic leaves are carried on rather straggling stems,
and the large golden flowers are arranged in loose clusters. Grows in
open woodland and shrubby areas in the far S.W. of Spain. (Sierra de
Ronda) *February–April.*

Viola cazorlensis

Family: *Violaceae*

With a very restricted range, confined to the Sierra Cazorla and a few neighbouring Sierras, this superb Violet is one of the gems of the Southern Spanish flora.

Growing on limestone scree at an altitude of 1500–2000 m., it makes loose cushions of 10 cm. stems, carrying small very narrow dark green leaves; the flowers are large, very long spurred and of a brilliant pink. Because of its great rarity and unique beauty, it is fortunate that most of the places where this violet grows lie within a forest reserve, where it is rigorously protected. (Sierra de Cazorla) *May–July.*

Nerium oleander (Oleander)

Family: *Apocynaceae*

A shrub with narrow leathery leaves, and erect stems up to 3 m. in height. The large and handsome flowers are carried at the ends of the branches, and vary from the more usual deep rose colour to pink or white. Often cultivated, but widely naturalized in dry sandy or gravelly places or along stream and river borders. (Granada) *April–September*.

Cistus monspeliensis

Family: *Cistaceae*

A sticky and very aromatic shrub, with small dark-green, narrow leaves, rolled at the edges. The small white flowers are carried in clusters. Grows, often in immense numbers, in the garigue of the Western Mediterranean. *March–June.*

Astragalus lusitanicus (Iberian Milkvetch)

Family: *Leguminosae*

A bushy and branching Vetch, reaching a height of up to 90 cm., with leaves divided into 14–20 ovate leaflets, and carrying dense axillary clusters of large cream coloured flowers with reddish calyces. Grows in rocky places, often in Cistus "Matorral". (Badajoz) *February–May*.

Convolvulus althaeoides

Family: *Convolvulaceae*

A trailing plant, often scrambling through low shrubs and herbage. Leaves heart-shaped and segmented. Flowers large, purplish pink, but darker in the throat. A common and beautiful flower of sandy places, hills and roadsides. (Merida) *April–June.*

Lithospermum purpureo-coeruleum (Blue Gromwell)

Family: *Boraginaceae*

A prostrate plant sending up short erect flowering stems. The leaves are narrow, dark green and hairy, and the flowers of an intense blue, carried in clusters. Grows in woods and shady places, usually on calcareous soils. (Picos de Europa) *April–June.*

Anthyllis cytisoides

Family: *Leguminosae*

A low shrub up to 80 cm. in height, with grey-green leaves and stems which carry loose spikes of lemon-yellow flowers with large green bracts. Leaves simple or trefoil. A handsome plant of the Western Mediterranean region, growing on steep rocky hillsides and cliffs not far from the sea. (Andalucia) *February–April.*

Ulex minor (Dwarf Furze) Right: **Rosmarinus officinalis** (Rosemary)

Family: *Leguminosae*

A common Gorse of Western Europe, with smaller flowers than the common Gorse. Grows on stony ground, hillsides, and in waste places. (Andalucia) *January–June*.

Spartium junceum (Spanish Broom)

Family: *Leguminosae*

This, the well-known Spanish Broom, grows to a height of up to 3 m. On its many erect almost leafless stems of a greyish-green colour, the large handsome golden flowers are carried in terminal spikes. Widely distributed, but preferring calcareous soils. (Andalucia) *May–July*.

Echium lycopsis (Purple Viper's Bugloss)

Family: *Boraginaceae*

Growing to a height of up to 1m., this common and handsome way-side flower has large oval leaves covered with soft hairs, and heads of blue-purple flowers. Of very wide distribution, this plant contributes much to the brilliant roadside colour of Spain from March to June. (Sierra de Gredos.)

Allium subhirsutum

Family: *Liliaceae*

A pretty and common Mediterranean Garlic with soft flat leaves and round heads of white flowers carried on cylindrical stems of up to 40 cm. height. Grows in dry stony places and on rocky hillsides. (Granada) *February–April.*

Ceratonia siliqua (Carob Tree, Locust Tree)

Family: *Leguminosae*

A characteristic tree of stony, rocky places on the Mediterranean, where its dense foliage of dark green leathery leaves provides shade for man and flocks. The flowers are inconspicuous but the fruit in long pods is used as food for farm animals. It reaches a height of up to 10 m. (Andalucia) *August–October*.

Prunus dulcis (Almond)

Family: *Rosaceae*

A small deciduous tree growing up to a height of 10 m. Leaves narrow
and lance-shaped. Flowers vary from white to deep pink in colour.
The Almond, originating in Western Asia, is widely cultivated and
often naturalized in the Mediterranean region of Spain and Portugal
where its flowers colour huge areas of hill and mountainside in
January and February. (Granada).

Asphodelus albus (White Asphodel)

Family: *Liliaceae*

A tall handsome Asphodel with long sword-shaped basal leaves, and flowering stems up to $1\frac{1}{2}$ m. in height, bearing a simple spike of large white flowers: sometimes there are a few short lateral branches below the main spike. Flower bracts brown.

A widespread and common flower in sandy or rocky places on the coast and inland. (Andalucia) *February–May.*

Leucojum trichophyllum

Family: *Amaryllidaceae*

This little plant, the most beautiful of all the Snowflakes, has 3 very narrow leaves, and flower stems of 10–20 cm. height which carry 1–4 drooping and bell-shaped flowers of white, often tinged with pink. This lovely little bulb is found here and there in Southern Portugal, the extreme S.W. of Spain, and in Morocco. (Andalucia) *January–April.*

96

Chrysanthemum hispanicum

Family: *Compositae*

A silky-haired perennial, with tufts of deeply cut leaves, and golden yellow flowers carried singly on stems up to 20 cm. in height.

A high mountain plant of the Spanish sierras, seen at its best on high screes where it forms compact and very floriferous clumps. (Sierra Nevada) *May–July*.

Cistus ladaniferus (Gum Cistus)

Family: *Cistaceae*

A tall-growing Cistus reaching a height of up to $1\frac{1}{2}$ m. The plant is sticky and aromatic, with narrow leaves dark green above and white below. The very large flowers, up to 10 cm. across, are borne singly and are white, with or without a purple blotch at the base of the petals. This species, perhaps the most handsome of all the Cistus genus, is widely distributed in Spain and Portugal, being generally found on acid soils. (Sierra de Gredos) *May–June.*

Narcissus nobilis

Family: *Amaryllidaceae*

This, the finest of the bi-coloured daffodils, grows to a height of 40 cm. and bears very large flowers with widely expanded golden trumpets and pale yellow twisted perianth segments.

It grows in high mountain pastures, often in wet boggy conditions, and has a wide distribution from Portugal through Galicia, Leon, Old Castille, and Asturias to the Central Pyrenees. (Huesca) *May–June*.

FRANCE

ASTURIAS

GALICIA

Picos de
Europa

BILBAO

LEON

Pyrenees

HUESCA

LÉRIDA
BARCELONA

R.Ebro

R.Duero

Sierra de
Guadarrama

Sierra de
Gredos

MADRID

R.Tagus

PORTUGAL

VALENCIA

R.Júcar

VALENCIA

LISBON

Serra
Arrabida

MÉRIDA

BADAJOS

SINES

Serra
Monchique

R.Segura

ALICANTE

R.Guadalquivir

ANDALUSIA

Sierra
Cazorla

SEVILLE

GRANADA

RONDA

MALAGA

Sierra Nevada

50   0   50   100   150
miles
km.
       50   0   50 100 150

NORTH

101

INDEX

The English names are given in italics

Acacia longifolia 51
Agave americana 20
Allium roseum 15
Allium subhirsutum 92
Almond 94
Aloe arborescens 61
Anchusa azurea 56
Anemone palmata 24
Angel's Tears 31
Anthyllis cytisoides 88
Arisarum vulgare 46
Aristolochia baetica 35
Arundo donax 76
Asphodel 57
Asphodelus aestivus 57
Asphodelus albus 95
Asphodelus fistulosus 14
Astragalus lusitanicus 85

Barbary Nut 23
Bermuda Buttercup 66
Blue Gromwell 87
Borago officinalis 53

Carob Tree 93
Carpobrotus acinaciformis 39
Carthamus arborescens 79
Century Plant 20
Ceratonia siliqua 93
Cercis siliquastrum 59
Chamaerops humilis 28
Chrysanthemum coronarium 78
Chrysanthemum hispanicum 97
Cistus ladaniferus 98
Cistus monspeliensis 84
Cistus populifolius 60
Common Borage 53
Convolvulus althaeoides 86
Convolvulus lanuginosus 49
Cork Oak 48
Crocus nevadensis 26

Crown Daisy 78
Cytisus multiflorus 80

Digitalis obscura 71
Dipcadi serotinum 16
Dwarf Fan Palm 28
Dwarf Furze 89

Echium lycopsis 91
Erica arborea 73
Erinacea anthyllis 27
Euphorbia characias 33

Friar's Cowl 46
Fritillaria hispanica 10
Fritillaria lusitanica 13

Gagea hispanica 11
Genista cinerea 32
Genista equisetiformis 58
Gentiana verna 25
Giant Reed 76
Gladiolus segetum 22
Gum Cistus 98

Halimium atriplicifolium 81
Hedgehog Broom 27
Helianthemum apenninum 44
Helichrysum stoechas 74
Hoop Petticoat Daffodil 63
Hyoscyamus albus 40

Iberian Milkvetch 85
Iris florentina 17
Iris planifolia 18
Iris sisyrinchium 23

Judas Tree 59

Lathyrus tingitanus 29
Lavandula dentata 37

Lavandula pedunculata 67
Leucojum trichophyllum 96
Lithospermum
    purpureo-coeruleum 87
Lobularia maritima 77
Locust Tree 93
Loose-flowered Orchid 43
Lupinus angustifolius 54

Matthiola sinuata 68
Medicago marina 62
Moricandia arvensis 64

Narcissus asturiensis 21
Narcissus bulbocodium 63
Narcissus bulbocodium var.
    citrinus 69
Narcissus minutiflorus 19
Narcissus nevadensis 34
Narcissus nobilis 99
Narcissus papyraceus 72
Narcissus triandrus 31
Nerium oleander 83
Nicotiana glauca 65

Odontosperum maritimum 75
Olea europaea 12
Oleander 83
Olive 12
Ononis natrix 55
Ophrys tenthredinifera 42
Opuntia ficus-indica 45
Orchis laxiflora 43
Oxalis pes-caprae 66

Paeonia broteroi 47
Palmate Anemone 24
Paper-White Narcissus 72
Phlomis purpurea 70

Pinus pinea 36
Prickly Pear 45
Prunus dulcis 94
Prunus prostrata 50
Purple Viper's Bugloss 91

Quercus suber 48

Ranunculus acetosellaefolius 30
Red Hottentot Fig 39
Rose Garlic 15
Rosemary 89
Rosmarinus officinalis 89

Sawfly Orchid 42
Scolymus hispanicus 41
Sea Medick 62
Sea Stock 68
Serapias pseudocordigera 38
Spanish Broom 90
Spanish White Broom 80
Spartium junceum 90
Spring Gentian 25
Stone Pine 36
Sweet Alison 77

Tangier Pea 29
Tree Heath 73

Ulex minor 89
Umbrella Pine 36

Vinca difformis 52
Viola cazorlensis 82

White Asphodel 95
White Henbane 40
White Rockrose 44